Skinny Dipping

Skinny Dipping

Suzanne Collins

Copyright © 2012 Suzanne Collins
All rights reserved

Palimpsest Press
5 King St, Kingsville, Ontario, Canada N9Y 1H9
www.palimpsestpress.ca

Book and cover design by Dawn Kresan. Typeset in Minion Pro, and printed offset on Rolland Zephyr Laid at Coach House Printing in Ontario, Canada.

Library and Archives Canada Cataloguing in Publication

Collins, Suzanne –
    Skinny dipping / Suzanne Collins.

Poems.
ISBN 978-1-926794-11-2

    I. TITLE.

PS8555.O4934S55 2012   C811'.6   C2012-904487-3

We thank the Canada Council for the Arts and the Ontario Arts Council for their support of our publishing program.

Canada Council for the Arts / Conseil des Arts du Canada

ONTARIO ARTS COUNCIL
CONSEIL DES ARTS DE L'ONTARIO

*For Friends and Family,
especially Matthew.*

Contents

I
What the fortune-teller told me   11
Why not   12
Grammar   13
Getting slicked up   14
Rumours about Nuns   15
Let me be flat and smooth   16
Screwball   17
The prophet's apprentice   18
Emily Carr's income house in Victoria, BC   19
Indian Church   20
Emily Carr on Spadina   21
My inner child is feral   22
Skinny Dipping   23
The Little Flower   24
Travelling with Thérèse   25
With Thérèse at the beach   26
The Wordsworths   27
Daffodils and Polaroids   28
Hot Knife   29
Mozzarella and the epic world   30
Pizza Eater   31
Stump   32

II
If Emily Carr were alive today   35
Emily is Loved   36
Diary of a cat sitter   37
Day in, day out   39
Reading Heidegger in bed   40
Emily Carr hums existence   41

The arbutus by moonlight   42
Bedtime   43
At the dream fields   44
Thresholds   45
Birthday   46
Roshambo at the all-night café   47
48 Times   48
Realpolitik Chicken Thursday   49
The name it hums   51
In Peace   52
Chacmool at the museum   53
Toward the hills   54
Their German Shepherd is friendly   55
Family and Friends   56
Night Walk   57

About the Author   59
Acknowledgements   59

I

What the fortune-teller told me

Hair waving like kelp,
fingers bejewelled with nematodes,
schools of fry swimming beside me;
I shall come up once again,
see low nimbostrata and cumuli above.
Brain synapses sizzle under a bone-hard
canopy. Jumbo words tip-toe to my fingers'
free margins, lunula and eponychium.
I'm claimed by welkin, not water's welter.

For—here's the prophecy—
I am a farmers' market
loose-gravel-road type
of person, with washboards and potholes
and narrow shoulders. Signage is minimal.
I shall take a long journey by land.

Why not

Because I opened the front door to daylight
and faux winter's dirty snow and icy puddles,
coat-wrestling & boot-tugging, I said, well, why not

sit awhile with my imaginary cat on my lap
reading about imaginary lives. Or go to a matinee
and come out, blinking like a mole,

and later a walk through a cemetery, stopping
at this or that stone to notice early dates & strange names,
the total of memories boxed up in big bones.

Why not spend a sprawled out evening,
TV screen between heart & feet & arms flung out,
sofa pillows propping up my heavy head.

Cat in, door locked. Lights out.

Grammar

This is about a verb and me,
and a grade nine English test I flunked

on the conjugation of the verb 'to be.'
Until then I didn't know verbs had moods.

A chocolate cake was sitting on the kitchen counter.
Nobody tasting it—what a shame.

I cut a generous piece across one end.
Dad was in the doorway.

Your mother baked that cake for her bridge club.
I wouldn't eat that if I were you.

I couldn't imagine Dad being me, or me, him.
I kept on eating the cake. I thought he was using

the subjunctive for a wish or a desire or a doubt.
Something contrary to fact. He cut the opposite end,

ragged and crumbly. I fixed that with a careful
quarter inch cut. He said he'd see that

and raise me another quarter inch.
Mother was now in the doorway.

I wouldn't do that if I were you—
It was intimation. A world of wishing

& wanting & waiting stretched before me.
Poised over the cake, Mother handed me the knife.

Getting slicked up

A boy swaggers from behind the garage,
a squawking hen under his arm.
He swings it overhead, then lays it
in a circle he's drawn in the dirt,
bang! the sun drops dead in its tracks.
Nothing moves until he yahoos.

Part one I already know—
the equipment needed to get slicked up.
Bottles, brushes, tubes
a home permanent kit smelling of ammonia,
nail polish redder than red, peroxide for streaks,
tweezers for an eyebrow to be raised.

A girl should twirl and spin
when she sits at the counter and sips a Coke,
oomphy in angora and accordion pleats,
feet swinging in classic penny loafers,
ready for part two, the fine side of the moon.
She has places of go, people to see, things to do.

Rumours about Nuns

If a kid did something
while Sister was writing on the board
out of nowhere would zoom a chalky eraser
and land—sometimes on the miscreant.
Rumours flew, the nuns were part alien.
A kid said he had seen them practicing shots
in the church basement—then they were gone
like a swirl of snow in a storm.
Their bodies were hidden, covered in heaps of cloth.
A black cape and veil over head and shoulders.
A long white robe and helmet-like cap. No hair.
Eyes, nose, mouth showed—the human part.
The alien part was under wraps.
Our grade eight Sister played softball with us.
She ran fast, robe billowing, veil flying,
rosary beads swinging from her brown leather belt.
Nobody challenged her on the base paths.
Before graduation, the grade eight girls
were invited to the convent house for tea.
A few of them thinking of becoming nuns.
Beige walls and no rugs. Not even a TV.
The nuns were cheerful anyway.

Let me be flat and smooth

If I were a stone, I'd be metamorphic.
Igneous is too original, sedimentary too easy.
Gneiss would be nice because it's taken for granite.
Let me be flat and smooth and skip over water.
Or, when galloping on a gnu,
contemplating gnostic notions,
how opportune, if push comes to shove,
that I fit a sling
and fell the goliath of the story we are in.

Screwball

Whiskey poured over ice becomes rocks
that sirens sit on and sing, *come here, come over here.*

I lull myself into the drink. I am practiced
and prepared for the trays of hors d'oeuvres,

the hordes, the habiliments. To the glass at my elbow
I say, "*Hello, hello, I am an ice cube,*" and I wink

which causes a crush all over the room.
The ice answers by snapping and splitting.

In many a glass a brave but futile sloshing
is all the response that can be given at the time.

Drinks are downed—or sadly neglected.
Through cigarette haze my free hand signals

the bartender—*hey, over here*—I hold up two fingers.
He winds up and delivers a round of screwballs

and a bucket of fresh ice.

The prophet's apprentice

The She who was a He
is old and sightless, does not deceive in prophecy.
Her fingertips play keys, doorknob, light switch—

something on her arm—
A chinch bug, I tell her. Nothing is sure, she says.
When we walk in the dew of near-night

I describe tree bats in flight, no small accomplishment.
It is not wise, she says, to let any one thing weigh too much.
She touches a withered breast, then beats the air.

Emily Carr's income house in Victoria, BC

Her tenants have iceberg lives.
Weighty masses moving in slippered shuffles,
blankets pulled tight against cold nights.
One-eighth shows above water—
a civility before rent is due and references
still believed. Below the water line lies
the rent-dodgers whose business it is
to remain hidden.

Through the door goes Emily who gulps
and digests the sticky mess of distrust.
She who needs the money, they who need
lodging. She who needs to paint, they who need
to put their heads down somewhere and dream.

In the parlour guardian angels exclaim,
Where does Central Casting get them?
And that landlady, whew.

Indian Church

Emily steps back,
one more stroke. It is good, this
painting of an Indian church on Nootka
in a clearing short distance from the road,

Primeval beak-shaped out-size leaves—
surround and threaten the Indian church,
a gliding menace squeezed from tubes.
Dip a brush in it and pull on the green.

The church has small spare white paint.
Door closed. A graveyard on one side.
But where are the people? Where is the narrative?
She puts down the brush, having perceived more

than she thought. Her feet on the threshold.
the fear of being locked out keeps the door closed.

Emily Carr on Spadina

Emily sees rock-hard-nosed buildings, streets swarming
with aspirants, tourists and vendors, rubbernecks and passers-by.

Children in muddy schoolyards devour recess.
Shoppers finger yard-long beans, hairy scarlet rambutan

bok choy, jicama, durian, bag loads to streetcars
dinging, grinding, clicking, swaying on the rails

She sees herself being flipped like a pancake
on a golden griddle floating above the

fried onions, boiled cabbage of the damn tenants
this way, that way, above the sizzle

a coming together of things, rocking and swaying
so that she sees now where streetcar lines lead

how and where she will get off
The sooner, the better, her feet hurt.

My inner child is feral

(though she's had expensive orthodontics)
snarls a smile through crooked teeth

at the accomplished, generalized me. Is
bleak eyed, easily spooked.

Jumps off my lap in a second
and speaks only two words, *Hello.*

Good-bye. Doesn't she want a home,
good china, conversation that gleams

like polished silver? Yet she's off—
passing a hand through candle flame,

stalking birds at the feeder,
lurking at other people's windows.

Skinny Dipping

The night came. The plan foolproof.
We went over the fence in groups of four,
helping each other, commando style.
No one was much surprised.
We had known naked bodies
for years in shared change rooms.
If caught, there was nothing the principal
could do to us. We were graduates,
floating under the stars.
The sheriff gave us a stern lecture,
told us to skedaddle after we lined up
to give our names and addresses.
Our parents were to be told.
We all knew there would never
be a second time.

The Little Flower

At school I had packs of baseball cards
and holy cards for trading. The jewel
of all my cards was St. Thérèse, *The Little Flower
of Lisieux*, holding an armful of roses.
I knew if I travelled far from home, the Thérèse card
would be in my backpack, for luck.
Rome had plenty of feral cats, swank shops and ruins.
The Pope at the Spanish Steps
in a red velvet cape trimmed in ermine,
white cassock. Red leather shoes,
designer sunglasses. *Viva Papa.*
At St. Peter's, rosaries held high sparkle
with the papal blessing. St. Thérèse would stay
this scene forever if she had a cloud to stand on.
She finds my backpack too crowded.
The thing about communion of this sort,
a dialogue now deemed highly improbable—
is that you are not alone.

Travelling with Thérèse

Wasn't easy. She lived her passion, suffering the ill will
of religious authorities. Rome denied her entry into the Carmelites

at age 15. Nine years later, dead at 24 from tuberculosis.
Quickly beatified and canonized. She was the people's saint.

A young nun precocious in image management.
In every Norman church, there she is

in her habit cradling huge bunches of roses, a crucifix
of suffering Jesus resting on the flowers. *Is that rose enough?*

She wrote that after her death she would send down showers
of roses. The promise became her message.

Her little way of smiling sweetly at Sisters she didn't like,
then offer it up to Jesus. That smile—a rose shot from a cannon.

With Thérèse at the beach

Bella Italia, when we tire of looking
at your cities & monuments & art
we go to the beaches for a rest and a swim
in the wine-dark Adriatic.
Immortal skies shimmer on those waters.

Young men roam the beach
shouting, *English miss, we love you! We love you!
Kiss-kiss!* and stroll in our direction.

It bothers Thérèse that they think her *anglaise*.
They slither closer as we wiggle into swimsuits
under tent—sized beach towels. I tell her to ignore them.
She drops the towel and reaches into the bosom
of her swimsuit—a rosary. Looking like Brébuef
at his martyrdom, she loudly prays the beads in French.

The Wordsworths

Never one to skip breakfast, William tucks into
porridge, a plate of fry, bread and a mug of tea.
Thus fortified, he proposes a run to Tintern Abbey.
Sister Dorothy says wash-up can wait.

They run on footpaths along the Wye,
along hedgerows and meadows,
past simple rustic cottages like their own.
Now rocks, now a cataract in rugged verdure.
This is all in all, William says.
Dear William, my thoughts exactly, replies Dorothy.

A roe breaks from the bush and bounds away.
William muses that blessings ever multiply—
Dorothy, the roe, light-dappled leaves,
clouds of gnats, the sun spinning, then still—
all could be saved and stretched.

Time for elevenses. Thoughtful Dorothy
has carried trail mix in her knapsack.
A passing hermit invited to share their snack,
his untutored gratitude cheers them both.
Dorothy dips cold water from a stream
and hands it to William who drinks—
like a fledgling bird, she thinks.

Daffodils and Polaroids

Onto the bridge come Wordsworth and Coleridge,
'the two amigos,' and William's sister Dorothy,
walking sticks firing iambs and anapests.

Houp-la, says Coleridge, banging his stick
on a bridge rail, sounds stout feels hard
smells like coal tar looks yellow, eh Wordsworth?

He points his stick at masses of wild daffodils.
Wordsworth mutters, then shouts "*All in all*"
with gusto, attracting a family of trolls

under the bridge who join in, chanting
"*hey hey hey—all in all—this happy day.*"
The trolls take Polaroid snapshots.

The one with the glittering eye and skinny hand
who stays your departure is
Coleridge, known to the trolls as Mr. C.

Hot Knife

A drive to Xanadu seems on the cards today
as daylight zooms through the windows.

A loud thump—someone passing has aimed
and tossed yesterday's news at the door.

I open the other eye. Today I shall avoid queues,
find loop holes, shortcuts, breaks in traffic.

Thinking of the car, I roll out of bed.
I'll hold the wheel delicately.

Le car, c'est moi. I'm alive and well
and cutting butter with a hot knife—

even though, I confess, the car isn't mine,
it's my dad's I don't know where Xanadu is.

Not in Canada. Must be somewhere romantic
where knives are hotter and butter not as cold as here.

Mozzarella and the epic world

Cut from the heel of work, I stop for pizza,
take a number and sit down—daydream

the bloody shores where a crowd of Trojans lead
a huge wooden contraption from the beach into the city.

They will celebrate this gift from the Greeks,
an expensive gift. Troy will burn to the ground.

A Trojan prince will escape, bearing his
aged father and household gods on his back,

his young son by the hand. The Trojan prince will found
an empire based on his mother's recipe for pizza.

Pepperoni will sizzle, dark-eyed olives
wink. It was fated.

Pizza Eater
(after Eric Fischl's painting, 1982)

The way the painter tells the story
a young girl wanders nude on a beach
drinking Coke and eating pizza,
not unaware that men are watching her,
a barefoot colossus aged ten or eleven.

You the viewer may see your own
stumbling emerge from the sand dunes,
buried pirates' gold or an unwanted corpse.
Something hidden on a Caribbean island.
"*Gimme a bite and a swig*" it would say.

Really it's just appetite beginning the chase,
digging toes in the sand, running hard.

Stump

It occurs to me—I am doing a foolish thing hacking at the box elder stump with an axe. I know the script and tools demanded—saw, kerosene, axe. Next summer a swath of grass will cover all this. Where you now see flickering blue flames, not a trace of this summer.

II

If Emily Carr were alive today

She would be a hunger artist
performing at malls and food courts.
People would gather to hear her stories
of a life lived in art; including the pinch.
and jab of poverty.
—and she does not eat. They watch her NOT
eat. They pay to watch.
O where is that line no one wants to fall below?
Her body aches, muscles are weakening.
Voice lies at the bottom of the teapot.
The hungrier she gets, the more she thinks
she smells bacon & eggs & coffee.
She can't see it but is convinced it is part
of the fugue she hears.

Emily is Loved

Emily Carr sells some paintings, buys a luxury item radio.
Static like ruckling, a grater pulled over a piece of satin.

Let's say it is a nutmeg grater and we know nutmeg attracts
ghosts who ordinarily would do something else.

Vincent van Gogh wasn't your typical ghost. What waved him on
was the sound of Emily's painting, her soul in the brushwork—

greenery growing, roots shaking, branches craving
sky. *My my*, he said, *that gal really has a way with a brush.*

He stops over. They fiddle with the dials.

Diary of a cat sitter

Friday (7:03 pm – 8: 30 pm)
Tillie shyly greets me. Not as outgoing
as Chester (RIP). I miss him already.
Read aloud the note you left.
Tillie loved it. She is on the table
as I write. Highlight—she purrs
when I pet her. Gave her a few Kittykisses
from the box on the counter.

Saturday (7:00 am – 1:25)
A hot and humid day, but the house is cool.
Paper brought in. Tillie saunters by, yawning.
I moved the flowers to the top of the china cabinet
because Tillie insists on eating fern parts.
She has fresh food & water, bowls washed.
Litterbox scooped. Tillie keeps her distance.
I offer a toy mouse, disdain. Then catnip
stuffed toy. Nix. Is she miffed re ferns?
The Kittykiss box is empty now.

Sunday (1:30 pm – 3: 30 pm)
Rain, a steady drizzle. Flowers watered.
Tillie creeps upstairs. Food hardly touched.
I read newspapers aloud to her. She yowls.
True, the papers have been unsettling lately.
I take down the anthology of Eng Lit.
She hops onto my lap. I read, *All discord,*
harmony not understood.
All partial evil, universal good.
One truth is clear—whatever is,

—Tillie is purring full throttle—*is right.*
When I start Eliot, she walks
across some 'Wasteland' pages
and makes for the basement.
Who can fathom the mind of a cat?
I shout to her, *They're back tonight.*

Day in, day out

They drag themselves out of bed
to the closets for school clothes. They eat
if there is time, rub their eyes.
Another ordinary boring day at school?

Staying home has certain conveniences.
Who can doubt the durability
of the Flintstones?

Imagine hundreds of thousands of years ago,
life in the trees—you wake up hungry
so you drop down a few branches
to the kitchen where Mom has stashed
berries, nuts and bananas.

You eat
hanging from a branch. Then swing over
to check on older brother, grooming
for lice and ticks. He's going out
on the savannah to hunt meat with the men.

Visiting the zoo on the next possible day,
none of us can imagine it, so remote,
so humbling, so sore are we that
we nearly forget we are sitting
in the shadow of the golden arch—

next to the cage of cousin Fred, the ape,
a recently discovered distant relative.

Reading Heidegger in bed

On the way to sleep I see a door and walk out into the rain. Mother catches up, chides me for being careless. Proof is that old sweater I am wearing, frayed & baggy & surely I don't have to carry a book (this time, Heidegger). I agree, but as she speaks again, rain dissolves her. Gone. It is interesting but not unusual for admonition to be washed away. I open the book, read that dread reveals nothing but Dread. Totality has flown out the window. This book is too heavy for me. I give up caring to know anything but rain and the smell of wet wool.

Emily Carr hums existence

A certain joy is behind cupboard doors
taken out on rare occasions by the old lady in the van
who sits on her stoop pencil and paper in hand
observing nature *out there* rolling along,
a river of it giving. O she hums while she works
knowing life is sometimes softened by
the strokes of a paint-laden brush, some compensation
for rain barrels brimming over with pain.
Faraway thunder, raw umber and episodes of
sienna steady the ochres, the blues, the greens.
Big wet drops fall. She retreats into the van,
hums. Tomorrow will be greener than today.

The arbutus by moonlight

Still and shadowed, Emily stands
outside herself, looking in at Emily
picking a windfall of bark twigs
and curls. Next day's work, weaving a cloth
for the grave that will receive her 3XL body.

The public Emily is scared. The one inside
goes calmly on her way. Scarcely notices
a small group of men, seven of them,
from the corner of her eye. They are not impressed,
No!—they wring their hands—*Too provincial.*
What they mean is "paint like us."

Which leaves Emily cold until an arbutus tree
bows to allow her to reach the higher bark.
A strange orange, middling red, rich fudge red.

She will set up her canvas. Watch for
people who sigh loudly but don't dream forests.
Let them enjoy, if nothing else, their copious
abundances. She will stay with her dream,
her shroud cloth, sew herself in.

Bedtime

This time it's Ludwig Wittgenstein for bedtime reading, lighter than Heidegger who said too much about Dread. I read & dozed. Wittgenstein and his students walk footpaths along the Cam. Here's the hypothesis: If Wittgenstein were to fall into the river, who would have pushed him? And why? Psychological vexation? Scholarly irritation? Teachers standing on riverbanks only net fish. Good teachers get wet. Great teachers drink hemlock. They disappear and let their students get on with it. Witty resembles a student's father—reason enough for an Oedipal shove? Witty thinks Freud a mere describer, a ransacker of mythology, a purveyor of bawdy outlines. Or, try a bucolic scene. A student points to it, loses balance, falls into the river taking Witty with him, like Keystone cops. Witty surfaces and sputters, *All motives are equally correct.* Little Tommy Flynn pushed him in. Johnny Stout pulled him out.

At the dream fields

Forms filled out, the sleeper
is asked routine questions:

On which field will your dream be born?
Are you ready for REM *sleep?*
How long are you usually awake at night?
Do you have anything to declare?
I hand over a passport in black and white.

Streaming over the fields are happy-go-gaudy
comic book colored creatures eager to
capture a caption and visit the Throne of Spin.

Every thing is allowed, even rhyme—
The fields are a riot of laughter and tears,
grunts, sleep talking and walking,
grinding teeth. The noise of dreams
being expanded and contracted is
as ponderous as cathedral doors shuddering,
or a retractable dome roof opening over
a baseball field—preludes
to judgment, history and today's score.

Sometimes dreams metastasize.
No cancer, but links of harrow
and harmony before exiting.

I dreamed I lost my wedding ring,
a gold band, at the A&P potato bin.
Frisking potatoes was not my thing.
So I was relieved to wake up
and find it on my finger.

Thresholds

The professor arrives, opens his briefcase.
Yes, lunch and sport clothes
but where are his lecture notes?

Children sing and dance
in a school play before a
bed sheet curtain. Wild applause.
Bravo, progeny.

A woman at the window—
curtains open to daylight.
She feels dusted with residue.
Who would have thought the night so dense?

Gold
$1800 an ounce
Coins or bars

A woman at the door—
a mask better covers what she believes
is written on her face. The rest of her body
apologizes at the threshold.

Birthday

She strikes a Spanish dancer pose,
does a turn with the scarf just unwrapped.
Around the table, applause. A mother dandles her baby
on her knee. The baby knows that mimicry
is the way to get noticed and shows a drooling hilarity
when we sing Happy Birthday.

The dancer twists the scarf through her fingers
Into a rope, has a tug of war between herself
and herself. She is definitely having a birthday.

Chocolate cake is served, a bite for Baby
whose eyes shine with new awareness.
When baby fists bang the table for more,
I wonder if he will become a politician?
His bib is drool-damp and chocolate smeared.
The scarf hangs about the dancer's neck.

Roshambo at the all-night café

Regulars hang out
at the corner of Free Will
and Fate—which to take?

At the front counter
hands make fists playing the game,
Rock—Paper—Scissors

A pair of scissors
snips close to the nape of thought,
too close for comfort.

Chiseled in stone—so
two can sit cheaply as one
in a dark back booth.

Seems there's no time like
the present to get tense in.
I am Who-Am-I?

Water is free here.
Counter ketchup poured in it,
cold tomato soup

Free of old men's guilt,
There's one axiom to hold.
Don't pass by anything.

48 Times

A poet-friend e-mailed me
a poem of chickens, pigs, and people,
challenged me to transmogrify. When peckish
I feel owlish & hunt the woods of labyrinthine
looks with soulful Bette Davis eyes.
Like an owl, I eat small prey
chew each bite 48 times,

spit out the lines,
getting short,
shorter,
until
only
whoo!

Realpolitik Chicken Thursday

The boy advertises himself as a magician, a Houdini
of the hen house who can make a chicken talk.
He works a downtown corner that attracts tourists.

Most don't believe him, but it is easier to
go along with it and see what happens.
He grabs a hen by her legs, swings her around,

lays her down in a magic circle he's chalked
on the sidewalk. Chicken Thursday doesn't move.
The boy claims she's hypnotized.

He claps his hands and stunned, she gets up.
He puts her next to him on a bench.
Her speaking voice is not pleasant.

She sounds like potatoes being mashed
in a metal pot. Thick and solemn.
Trains, she told us, steam in and out of tunnels

with foodstuffs and supplies for *The End* of the world.
But nothing's perfect. Chicken Thursday hops off
the bench and mutters something about discontent.

Then to the boy she shouts, "Why didn't I see it?
This speech is yours, not mine.
Those are your words, you fraud."

The boy defends himself, "You will never utter
another syllable." She avoids his grasp and runs.
He follows, shouting for her to stop.

She runs through the first open door.
A restaurant hostess greets her,
"the kitchen is at the end."

The name it hums
>(for H.E.C who died in a farm accident)

    Some say Fate did it. The young man riding
    a lawn mower, a chariot from Corinth
    along the lane from his farm home.
    Dust flew into his eyes
    as he turned onto the road
    at triple junction.
    The machine rolled over

    He died instantly
    of multiple injuries,
    and the machine landed
    on its wheels. The chariot sped on
    The body carried home
    causes sought, reason ended
    simply: the young man himself, the machine
    out of his control. What more?
                         unless an answer
                         be made art
    and death outdone in the saying
    of the name it hums, running smoothly, indefinitely.
    But then he would have to be
    other than what he was,
    an ordinary son strangely uncut
    by the blades of the machine.

In Peace

Cemetery stroll,
sparrows fly through the link fence
we must walk around.

Someone remembers.
Bunch of pink plastic flowers,
the kind ghosts admire.

Cemetery smile.
A pile of fresh-cut tree-ends,
Basho's 'moon tonight.'

Certain dangers then,
a soldier at Vimy Ridge,
women in childbirth.

Scarcely legible,
children under limestone stubs
too weathered to read.

Only transients,
genealogists, sad sacks
like me read gravestones.

An understatement—
that the quiet is quiet,
this common dust, ours.

Chacmool at the museum

The guard gives me a look that says, *don't touch.*
A railing guarantees that.
The untouchable one is reclining on his elbows
As if sunning at a beach, watching girls.
The kind of figure you'd like to run your fingers over,

rub sun tan lotion on his back. But remember, he's
stone, a life-size guardian of a Mayan-Mexican shrine
holding a plate for sacrifice, human and animal.
Can't you see the carnage in the corner?
This chacmool need only rest on his elbows.
Your imagination does the rest.

Toward the hills

Not this hill. Not that hill. But all the hills
your eyes have lighted on. Loved ones
are riding toward those hills, floaters
wandering from the lining of an eye.

Their German Shepherd is friendly

Tonight the bedroom across the street has open curtains.
Some sort of tapestry hangs on the wall over their bed.
A lamp on the table by their bed glows.
I have lived opposite those people for thirty years
of mowing lawns, sharing grass-growing strategies,
taking out garbage, tending flowers,
going to block parties where we drink beer and have opinions.
I stand by my window and look into theirs.
Do they, like me, think love grows greener
across the street?

Family and Friends

A scientist-friend explains why
birds flit back and forth,
feeder to bush, bush to feeder.
They are chased by ghosts of predators
long ago, swooping down on them,
beaks and rapier-like talons,
napkins flapping.

At this time of year
when everything's frozen,
feed your stale bread
to our duck brothers and sisters
crossing the ice
swimming
in narrow channels of water.
Each should get a piece,
even the ugly ones.

I light candles and set the table.
As I am ladling soup, ghosts appear—
and in sipping voice
chorus how much they would like some.

Night Walk

So I walk from circle to circle of street light—
on asphalt still fuelling the gas-fired grid
of the city, a barefoot night chaser after
the longest, hottest day on record—

when a boy in a swim suit shouts
something in my direction as he runs by
without pause and turns a corner. Gone.
Leaving me alone on the street.

Something disarming about tonight's moon.
Well, it's the old man and the cows
that give us leave to push back the darkness
with stories the stand against time.
Must be what the boy was shouting about.

About the Author

Suzanne Collins has been called a "late bloomer" by critics. Her first book, *Wonders at the Corner*, was published after she retired from her lengthy career as a university instructor. Her work has also appeared in *Poetry as Liturgy: An Anthology by Canadian Poets*. She lives in Toronto, Ontario, with her husband.

Acknowledgments

Earlier versions of these poems have appeared in *The Antigonish Review*, *Jones Ave*, *Contemporary Verse II*, *Raw Nervz*, *Sign and Symbol*, and the anthology *Poetry as Liturgy: An Anthology by Canadian Poets*.

A series of Emily Carr poems was long listed for the CBC Literary Awards in 2008.